Frenchie
Kisses

For Lily, my little rat

Frenchie Kisses

The Many Faces of the French Bulldog

Photographs by **Amanda Jones**

B

berkley books, new york

THE BERKLEY PUBLISHING GROUP
Published by the Penguin Group
Penguin Group (USA) Inc.
375 Hudson Street, New York, New York 10014, USA
Penguin Group (Canada), 90 Eglinton Avenue East, Suite 700, Toronto, Ontario M4P 2Y3, Canada
(a division of Pearson Penguin Canada Inc.)
Penguin Books Ltd., 80 Strand, London WC2R 0RL, England
Penguin Group Ireland, 25 St. Stephen's Green, Dublin 2, Ireland (a division of Penguin Books Ltd.)
Penguin Group (Australia), 250 Camberwell Road, Camberwell, Victoria 3124, Australia
(a division of Pearson Australia Group Pty. Ltd.)
Penguin Books India Pvt. Ltd., 11 Community Centre, Panchsheel Park, New Delhi—110 017, India
Penguin Group (NZ), 67 Apollo Drive, Rosedale, North Shore 0632, New Zealand
(a division of Pearson New Zealand Ltd.)
Penguin Books (South Africa) (Pty.) Ltd., 24 Sturdee Avenue, Rosebank, Johannesburg 2196,
South Africa

Penguin Books Ltd., Registered Offices: 80 Strand, London WC2R 0RL, England

The publisher does not have any control over and does not assume any responsibility for author or third-party websites or their content.

PRINTING HISTORY
Berkley hardcover edition / January 2005
Berkley trade paperback edition / July 2010

Berkley trade paperback ISBN: 978-0-425-23441-9

The Library of Congress has catalogued the Berkley hardcover edition as follows:

Jones, Amanda.
Frenchie kisses : the many faces of the French bulldog / photographs by Amanda Jones.
    p. cm.
ISBN 978-0-425-20214-3
1. French bulldog—Pictorial works. I. Title.
SF429.F8 J66 2005
636'.72—dc22   2004060576

PRINTED IN THE UNITED STATES OF AMERICA

10 9 8 7 6 5 4 3 2 1

Acknowledgments

During the creation of this book, certain people helped in extraordinary ways, and I owe them a special thank-you:

To all of the French Bulldog models and their passionate owners who took time out to work with us;

To Allison McCabe's constant enthusiasm and support;

To Julie, David, and Harry for graciously sharing their home during my busy New York trips;

Of course to Chris and Sophie who make this all worthwhile.

Attitude is a little thing
that makes a big difference.

—SIR WINSTON CHURCHILL

I like the smell of clover,
it makes me roll over.

There's a funny aroma right here on the ground.

But I *can't* tell you what it is—
did you think I was a hound?

Rub my belly.

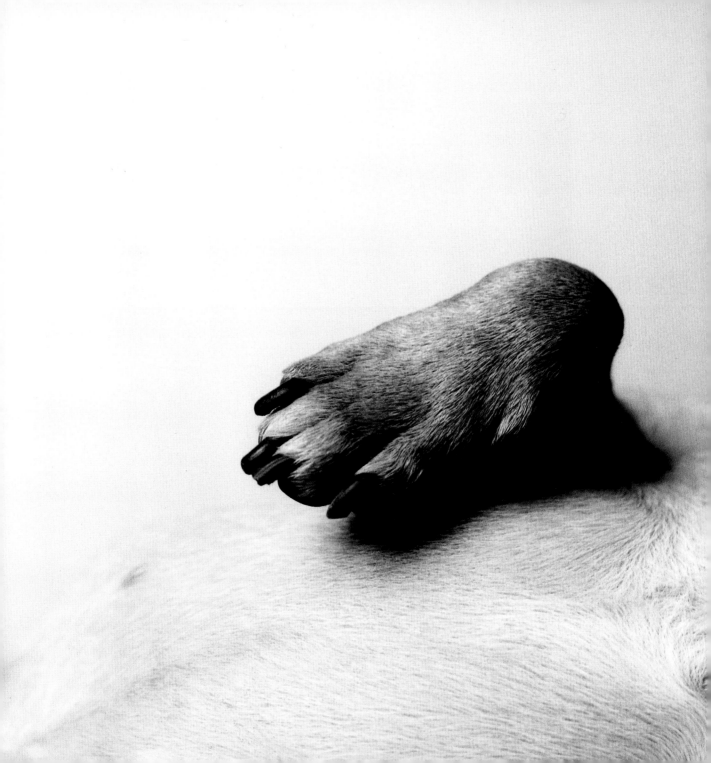

Squirting the hose is always fun.

Shake the water from your nose when you're done.

Black on White

White on Black

The treats are in the bag.

Pass it on.

I know where the treats are!

Really.

Hey! Wait for me!

Bulldogs are adorable,
with faces like toads that have been sat on.

—COLETTE

A real pisser.

I'm a mighty hunter—

Call me Frog Dog!

Heaven goes by favor.
If it went by merit,
you would stay out
and your dog would go in.

—MARK TWAIN

Go for a walk, did you say?

"Whisker"

"Wrinkle"

Meet you halfway . . .

But if you snooze, you lose.

Only mad dogs and Englishmen
go out in the midday sun.
—NOËL COWARD

It's not always easy being a puppy.

But I do my best.

I'm adorable.
No butts about it.

Pick me! No me!
Me, me, me!

How can you pick just one?

Imagine what I would see . . .

. . . if only I could get up this tree.

No animal should ever jump up
on the dining-room furniture
unless absolutely certain
that he can hold his own
in the conversation.

—FRAN LEBOWITZ

I'm *not* a Boston Terrier.
Honestly, I'm asked that all the time.

H*iiiii*-YAH!

It's a fact,
and hard to ignore . . .

When we sleep,
we sometimes snore.

I thought I was lucky
to get near this ducky.
Now it's hard to tell.
My fur's all wet—
do I smell?

My little dog, a heartbeat at my feet.

—Edith Wharton

L'amour . . .

n'a pas de prix!

Are you talkin' to me?

Puppy Love

We know we're cute, okay?
Put the camera away.

Smiling, our tongues reach our chins.
But here's something not everyone knows . . .

If we flip back our heads
they can touch our nose!

Jump!

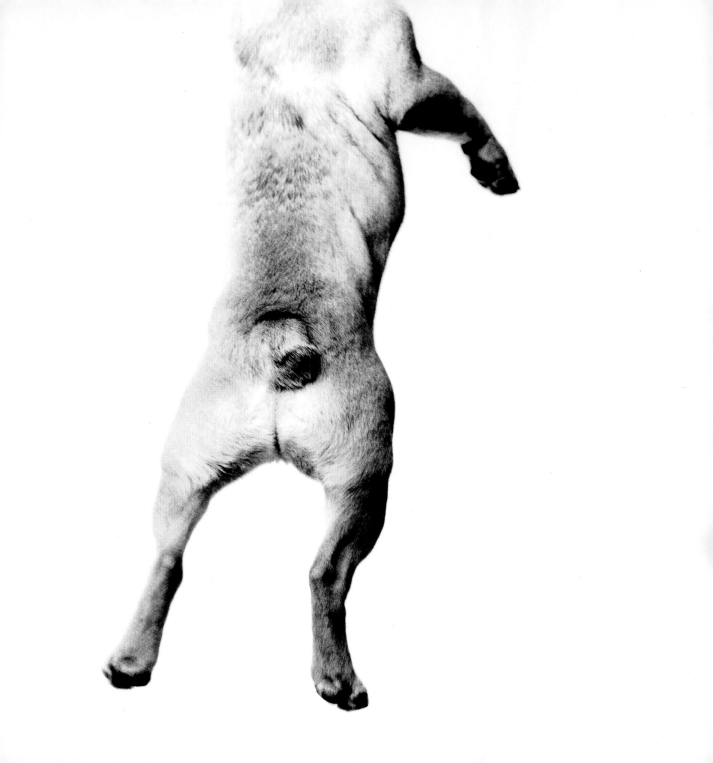

The language of friendship is not words

but meanings.

—HENRY DAVID THOREAU

When you're away . . .

I wait for you.

That squirrel will *never* come down.

Or will it?

I admit it; it was me.
Beans and I do not agree.

Your face is a book,
where men may read strange matters.

—WILLIAM SHAKESPEARE

To be able to fill leisure intelligently
is the last product of civilization

and at present very few people have reached this level.

—BERTRAND RUSSELL

Oh! Was that *your* dinner?
It was delicious.

I'm ready for my close-up!

Thanks to the following Frenchies (and their humans!) who participated in this project:

Rosco
Tallulah
Delphine & Dedier
Franklin & Rodney
Clarisse
Xena, Elmo, & Cher
May
Mini, Jade, Pete, & Mieke
Harry
Josephine
Pitou, Beano, Bibbitt
Indie
Maddy
Chesty, Bivwac, Bellfao, Gunny, Cadence, Junie, Recon, & Diva
Gable
Dao
LaRoux
Sophie
Bean
Oscar, Charlie, Rose, Luke, & Pace
Milo

If you are thinking of bringing a Frenchie into your life, go online and read about them on the various websites dedicated to these dogs, to make sure that a French Bulldog is a good fit for your lifestyle. Below are two sites you may want to visit:

French Bulldog Club of America Rescue League
www.fbdcarl.org

French Bulldog Rescue Network
www.frenchbulldogrescue.org